DIBS AND DABS
of MY LIFE

Gertrude Coulter

WESTBOW
P R E S S®
A DIVISION OF THOMAS NELSON
& ZONDERVAN

WestBow Press books may be ordered through booksellers or by contacting:

WestBow Press
A Division of Thomas Nelson & Zondervan
1663 Liberty Drive
Bloomington, IN 47403
www.westbowpress.com
1 (866) 928-1240

ISBN: 978-1-5127-7029-2 (sc)
ISBN: 978-1-5127-7028-5 (e)

Library of Congress Control Number: 2016921471

Print information available on the last page.

WestBow Press rev. date: 1/5/2017

To my children and grandchildren,

with love

I believe that I grew up in the best of times: anyone could walk around the block after dark without feeling afraid; most children lived in two-parent homes; children walked to neighborhood schools; life was family-oriented; and mothers were stay-at-home moms.

"Oh no, what am I going to do with three boys?" my father remarked when the nurse told him twin boys were on the way. Yet the nurse was mistaken. On March 15, 1927, at Baptist Memorial Hospital in Memphis, Tennessee, my mother did give birth to twins, but they were a boy and a girl. I am that girl, Gertrude Ellen Shapard. My twin brother, James Edward Shapard, came into this world weighing over fifteen pounds. That birth was the beginning of a restless, busy, and exasperating life for the family, taking care of us and my older brother, Roy Thomas Shapard Jr. Roy was two years nine months at the time, only a baby himself. After two weeks in the hospital, we went home to my grandmother and grandfather's house at 1651 Evelyn in Memphis. It took the entire family to take care of us. This was the beginning of a very happy and satisfying life that changed drastically during the following years.

Roy Jr. and the twins

Grandmother and Granddaddy Plumlee lived in a two-bedroom, one-bath house. We had five in our family, which made a total of seven people in that house. It was not unusual for married children to live with their parents until they could afford a home of their own.

There was a swing across one end of our porch, and we used to love to sit out there and swing. Since there were no air conditioners, we stayed on the porch quite a bit in the warm weather. Even though we lived in the city, Granddaddy had a chicken yard in the back and raised chickens to eat and to have their eggs. When we wanted fried chicken for dinner, Grandmother would go out to the chicken yard, catch a chicken, and wring its neck. It took a certain skill to hold the chicken by the neck and twist it 'round and 'round until the chicken would go flying across the yard, and she would still be holding the chicken's neck in her hand. It took a certain twist of the wrist to attain that skill. Then the chicken would flop around and around on the ground until its last breath left its body. Grandmother would pick it up and take it in the house, where a pot of boiling water was waiting to scald the chicken so the feathers could be removed with ease. After removing the feathers, she would hold the chicken over the fire to singe it. After taking the insides out, she would cut it up; then it was ready to fry. Having fried chicken was quite an ordeal but also a treat for the family.

Granddaddy Plumlee and Roy Jr.

The Plumlee family reunions were always so much fun. My family would get up early and, with our potluck, drive a hundred miles to Clarendon, Arkansas. Every July 26 my grandfather Plumlee and his four brothers had a family reunion in Clarendon, where they were born. Three of the brothers still lived there, and one brother lived on the farm where their parents had once lived and farmed.

The old clapboard farmhouse where Uncle Rob and

3

Aunt Minnie lived had a vine-covered front porch and a back porch. There were chairs set up in the yard. Wooden sawhorses with boards on top were the tables. Everyone would bring their favorite dishes, so there was always lots and lots of food. We seemed to eat all day. We saw people we only saw once a year.

Plumlee Reunion 1928

One year the reunion was by the river. Everyone drove on a dirt lane through a cotton field until they reached the banks of the White River. There were no facilities, so the women would spread quilts on the ground for our tables and would put all of our food on the quilts. On one occasion after lunch, the five Plumlee brothers decided they would drive to town. As a child, I had no idea why they chose to do this, but the spouses knew why they made the trip

After being gone for some time, we looked up and saw them coming through the cotton field in their dark green 1927 Chevrolet sedan. The car stopped—then it went a little farther and stopped again. I had no idea what was going on, but Aunt Lucille did. She always talked in a definite, emphatic tone. I can just hear her now saying, "Those old drunks." Sure enough, when they finally got back to the riverbank, it was clear they had been drinking. I don't think they were drunk, but they had been celebrating.

When Jim and I were about three years old, my family moved into our own house at 2377 Lamar, which was in the county at the time. It was a red brick two-bedroom house with one bath. As you came in the back door, there was a small entrance just large enough for an icebox. Every day the ice man would come and leave ice. There was a compartment in the top of the icebox that held the ice, with a drain that ran down to the bottom of the box. A container was put under the drain to catch the water as the ice melted. We had to check every so often to be sure it did not run over. The ice would last until the next day. I don't know what we did on Sundays, but we seemed to survive.

I remember the day we got an electric refrigerator. It was a Norge and was quite small compared to the refrigerators of today. We bought it from Pearce's Hardware Store on Lamar. How excited we all were when the box was delivered. One of the first things Mama did was to make ice cream. She found a recipe for ice cream that could be made in the ice trays. That was quite a novelty, but it turned out not to be as good as the freezer ice cream, where you had to turn the crank, so we went back to turning the crank. It was the kids' job to sit on the top of the freezer when the ice cream started getting hard. I never was heavy enough to make a difference, so the boys got the sitting job.

Jessie May Bridgeforth was our maid for several years—from the time I was about three years old until I was about ten or eleven years old. I think she has earned an article in this book. At the time, we had no washing machine or dryer. Jessie May would come every Monday to do the wash. She would use two big washtubs filled with water. They were put on a wash bench in the backyard. She would scrub the clothes on a scrub board in one tub and rinse them in the other tub. Then she would hang them on the line to dry.

We were crazy about Jessie May. When I wanted my mother to fix me a cup of coffee, Jessie May would say, "If you drink that coffee, you will be black like me." Jessie Mae was going to Detroit for a vacation, and I wanted to make her some cupcakes to take on the bus. I worked all morning, got flour all over my dress (girls didn't wear pants then), and put the cupcakes in the oven. They didn't rise. I could not imagine what was wrong until I reread the recipe. I found that I had left out the eggs—so Jessie May went to Detroit without any cupcakes. She and her husband eventually moved to Detroit. She and my mother corresponded for years, until my mother was not able to write.

There was a porch across the front of our house with a swing at one end—like at Grandmother's. When we had company, we gathered on the porch. We had hanging wire baskets lined with moss across the porch front. We would go out into the woods and dig the moss from around the trees and also get some dirt, as that was supposed to be good rich soil. Mama would line the baskets with the moss, put the good rich soil on top of the moss, and then plant her flowers, usually petunias. The hanging baskets of today remind me of Mama's baskets, but we made our own instead of buying them already made.

Since our house had only two bedrooms, my brothers had one bedroom and my mother and daddy had the other. I was shifted around wherever there was a space. I slept on a day bed that was sometimes in the dining room and sometimes in Mama and Daddy's room. If the preacher was coming to dinner, my bed was moved to my parents' room. The back bedroom, which was the boys' room, had a huge walk-in closet with shelves on one side. We would stretch blankets from shelf to shelf and make a playhouse or a place to hide—at least we thought we were hiding.

Mama kept her sewing machine, a Singer treadle, in the bedroom, and I would stand on the machine and sing, mocking Bessie Mae Thomas. Bessie Mae sang in our church choir, which was directed by Mr. Henley. Bessie Mae had a beautiful voice and would sing solos at church. When she sang, Mr. Henley would stand in front and wave his hands around. So when we played church, I would stand on the machine with a book in hand and sing and sing and sing, and Jim would stand in front and wave his hands around like Mr. Henley.

Mrs. Chumney was our next-door neighbor. She started going to our Methodist church, even though she had always been a Baptist. After attending our church for some time, she decided to join, but for her baptism she wanted to be immersed instead of being sprinkled like the Methodists. Our minister used another church's baptismal, and one Sunday afternoon our church members attended the baptism of Mrs. Chumney. That was fascinating for my brothers and me. For weeks afterward, we must have been the most "baptized" children in the world. We would stand on the throw rug in front of the living room door (our baptismal) and Jim or Roy would put his right hand in the middle of my back, hold my nose with the other hand, and lean me backward as he said, "I baptize you in the name of the Father, Son, and the Holy Ghost. Amen." We did this over and over again for weeks.

We went to Rebecca Memorial Methodist Church, which was a fairly new church at the time. It was small and very simply decorated. It had an outside toilet and no kitchen facilities. In fact, it had the very minimum of facilities to still be called a church. But that was what made it so nice. Everyone was like family. We were at the church every time the doors opened.

I remember one Sunday when we took Grandmother and Granddaddy to Hot Springs, Arkansas, for an outing. When we got back, some of the church members told Mama that Brother Lewis had preached his sermon on the sin of members missing church to go out of town on a pleasure trip.

Brother and Mrs. Lewis were an elderly couple when they came to our church. They had no children, but Mrs. Lewis's old-maid sister lived with them. They had a maid who cleaned and cooked for them, and she cooked enough on Saturday to last through Sunday because the preacher did not believe in cooking on Sunday.

We were going to have chicken for dinner one night. Roy had seen my grandmother wring a chicken's neck so many times that he thought that he could do it. He did it just like Grandmother. He swung the chicken around and around and then let it go. However, it did not flop around on the ground. Instead, it got up and flew over the backyard fence and into the field next to our property. The entire family had to chase that chicken around the field before we caught it.

After we moved to our own house on Lamar, we would go back to Grandmother's about once a week and on Sunday for lunch. Grandmother was such a good cook, and of course she cooked everything from scratch. If we did not go to Grandmother's for Sunday dinner, we would get Grandmother, Granddaddy and Mamaw (Daddy's mother) and take them for a Sunday afternoon ride. It was a treat to stop somewhere and get a nickel drink.

My grandfather was an engineer for the Missouri Pacific Railroad. He worked at night, so he had to sleep during the day. One of the things I will always remember him saying is, "If you want to eat, you must work." He instilled a good work ethic in us. My grandmother was a housewife, as very few women worked out of the home at that time. Before she married, however, she had taught school. Schoolteachers were not allowed to be married, so when she got married, she had to quit teaching.

Grandparents Eddie and Mamie Plumlee

During the Depression, my daddy was laid off as a machinist for the Frisco Railroad. I knew nothing of the family finances because I was too young to understand. I do know that Daddy was not working, and he started raising chickens. He built chicken coops so that the chickens never touched the ground. He would sell live chickens to the grocery stores and to anyone else who could afford to buy them. I went with him to deliver the chickens and was fascinated by how the feathers were taken off. There was some kind of contraption that could whip off the feathers. This was our livelihood until the Frisco called Daddy back to work.

We always had food to eat. Food was so cheap that one would think that everyone could eat, but there were some who did not have enough money to buy food. People would go door to door, begging for food. When someone would come to our door, Mama would always fix a plate, and the person would sit on the back steps or the porch and eat. Bread cost five cents a loaf, eggs were twelve cents a dozen, and we could buy a week's supply of groceries for five dollars. That would feed our family of five as well as the beggars who came to our door.

Churches were a big help during the Depression. Mama visited one family that had no food and no sheets on the beds. Through the church, she bought them food, and someone furnished sheets and pillowcases. However, when Mama went back later to check on them and to see if they needed more food, they still did not have sheets on the bed and were in the same condition as they were the first visit.

We survived the Depression, and I am sure that we learned from the experience.

My mother was an only child, and our being the only grandchildren was to our advantage. With Grandmother, everything had to be equal among us three children. We had to take turns spending the weekend at her house, and for no reason could we get out of turn. She rarely got two of us at the same time—I don't blame her for that. Together, Jim and I could be a handful. One of the rare occasions when Jim and I were together at Grandmother's, we locked ourselves in the bathroom. Grandmother called Mama, but she didn't get any sympathy. Mama told her, "Just let them stay there." The thing about our being twins is that we were double trouble—whatever one of us didn't think of, the other one did, and we each would back the other.

One of the most interesting and enjoyable things that happened when we were at Grandmother's was seeing the organ grinder. This little old man would walk around making some kind of noise so that we would know that he was coming, and we would run to the porch. The organ grinder had a little monkey that he dressed up in finery, and the monkey would jump off the man's shoulder and do a little dance for us while the organ grinder played a little tune. After the monkey finished its presentation, it would hand us a cup, and we would put a nickel in it. It would jump back on the organ grinder's shoulder, and they would be on their way.

Another interesting event was when the market man would come down the street in a horse-drawn wagon. When Grandmother heard the sounds of the horse's hooves clomp, clomp, clomping down the street, we would go to the curb and see what the market man was selling that day. It would usually be fresh vegetables and fresh fruit. Grandmother would pick over the vegetables and buy enough for the next meal. Every morning Grandmother would order her groceries from the local grocery store or get them from the market man.

Every fall and spring Grandmother and Mama would take us three children to town (there were no shopping centers or malls), and Grandmother would buy our clothes for the coming season. We would go to Bry's Department Store because that was where Grandmother shopped. I think every sales clerk in the store knew her. As we went from department to department, the clerks would say, "Hello, Mrs. Plumlee." It would be an all-day affair, but I would come home with five or six dresses and accessories to go with them, a coat if it was fall, and shoes (one pair for school and one pair for Sunday). The boys would have outfits for school and Sunday. I can remember what an ordeal it was when the boys had to try on their suits. Of course, it seemed a long wait for me because I had already bought my clothes and just had to sit and wait on them. Between shopping for me and shopping for my brothers, we always had lunch. Since people did not eat out very often, it was a treat for all of us. This was also the only time during the year that my grandmother ate out.

Gertrude, Roy, and Jim—after spring shopping spree

At the age of six years, I asked my mother to teach me how to crochet—I not only asked but begged and begged until she finally gave in. Mom gathered the materials that I needed: thread, a size-eight crochet hook, and a rocking chair. The thread actually was cord that was wrapped around a stick that Jim and Roy used for flying kites. The first lesson was how to make a chain, the basic stitch for every crochet article. I sat in my chair and made chains over and over again. With this process, I finally had a chain that reached from my yard to my neighbor's yard— and there was a vacant lot in between. The entire summer, I made chains. When I was eight years old, I made my first crocheted article, a pin cushion for my mother's birthday. I worked on the gift for weeks and could hardly wait for her birthday. After my mother opened the present, and I told her what it was, she said in a very proud voice, "I just love it."

Jim and I started to school at Bethel Grove Elementary School. There was only one section per grade so that meant that Jim and I were in the same room. That worked pretty well after our teacher, Mrs. Bomar, put us at the same table. Our seating was arranged at large tables, according to our reading levels.

We had a thirty-minute recess in the morning. Boys and girls did not play together. There was a girls' side and a boys' side of the playground, and we did not cross the line. We played dodge ball and Red Rover; we jumped rope and played jacks. We got enough exercise that we did not need physical education classes.

Lunches cost a nickel, and we could buy a cookie for

an extra penny. Most of the time we brought our lunches to school wrapped in a newspaper; there were no such things as lunch boxes. My elementary school boyfriend would buy me a cookie and slip it in my desk. That same boy now eats lunch every fourth Monday with our graduating class.

When Jim and I were twelve years old, we moved to 3001 Lamar (Highway 78). Daddy was in the process of building our house, and we moved in before it was completed. My room was not finished, so I still slept on my cot in the dining room. That was okay since we were all so happy to be in our new home.

Every Monday was washday. We had graduated from a washboard to an electric washing machine with a wringer. It took at least a half day of continually working to set up for the wash, do the wash, and then clean up. Mama usually started by eight o'clock in the morning. She would roll the washer to the middle of the floor on the enclosed back porch. Then she'd place a wash tub at the end of the washer and another tub at the side of the washer.

After the equipment was set up, she had to fill the washer and tubs with water. She boiled water on the stove and carried it to the washer and tubs. She used the same water to wash all the clothes that we had worn the week before, plus linens, yet we were always clean. We had to have enough clothes to last us all week because we never washed clothes more than once a week.

After sorting the clothes in piles of white, dark, towels, and linens, she put them in the washing machine and washed each load for thirty minutes. There was no timer on the machine, so she had to watch the clock. After each thirty-minute washing cycle, she turned the wringer around so that it was over the first rinse tub and manually fed the clothes through the wringer so they fell into the rinse water. After rinsing the first tub of clothes by hand, she turned the wringer around to the second tub and filled that tub with clothes. After the second rinse, the clothes were ready to hang on the clothesline in the backyard. Even in cold weather, the clothes had to be hung outside. I can remember that at times in the winter, the clothes would freeze on the line.

When they dried, they were ready to iron. There was no such thing as no-iron materials; everything was 100 percent cotton, which made ironing a necessity. Early on Tuesday mornings, Mama would sprinkle all of the clothes and roll them in a towel, ready for ironing. Her sprinkler consisted of a Coke bottle with an attachment full of holes for sprinkling. I always wanted to help iron, but the only things that Mama would let me iron were the handkerchiefs and the men's underwear. Mama said that I wanted to help when I was too young, but when I was old enough to help, she couldn't find me. However, I did help with chores that fit my age.

When Jim and I were in the fifth grade, I contracted the red measles. At that time we were quarantined, which meant that Jim could not go to school if he stayed at home. The health department said that the measles germ could be carried through one's clothes. So Jim stayed at my grandparents', and they took him to school each day. I was so sick, with very high fever and a heavy red rash all over my body. I missed six weeks of school. As I was getting well, Jim came down with the measles, and I had to stay with my grandparents. Jim missed five weeks of school. This was years before the measles vaccine was developed.

We moved from Bethel Grove Elementary School to Oakville School when Jim and I were in the sixth grade. We attended that school through the eighth grade. We rode the bus to school except when it snowed; then we would walk to school just for fun. There would hardly be anyone in class on those days, so we had a good time. We would never think of walking that far any other time. Some of the friends that I made at Bethel Grove and Oakville are still friends.

From Oakville, we went to Whitehaven High School. When Jim and I were in the ninth grade, Roy was a senior. Whitehaven was a county school, and we had to catch the bus at 7:30 in the morning. We got home about 4:00 in the afternoon. I loved my high school days. We had a strict but very fair principal, Mr. Eliot. He thought that every student should be loyal to our school, so when Jim and I wrote a rinky-dink poem about the school, he thought that we were being disloyal to our school. For three days in a row, Jim pinned the poem to the bulletin board in the hall, and almost immediately, it would disappear.

One morning Mr. Eliot called all the boys into the auditorium and gave a long speech about loyalty to our school. After using a long list of negative adjectives about the person who had written the poem, he said, "Now let me see if the person that wrote that poem has the guts to stand up." That was all Jim needed. He stood up and was immediately sent to the office. Mr. Eliot said that if anyone helped him with the poem, Jim should go get that person. Jim came to the library where I worked that period and said, "Come on. We have to go to the office." He filled me in on the way. We were suspended for three days. Mama talked to Mr. Eliot that night, and he allowed us to return to school the next day. The following is a copy of the poem that got us suspended:

> There's lots you can't and not much you can
> So here's a list "man to man"
> You can't draw
> You can't chaw
> 'Cause they made the law.
> You can't draw on the wall
> You can't stand in the hall
> There's hardly anything you can do at all.
> You've got to be dry
> You can't lie
> 'Cause "Leaping Lena" is on the spy.
> You can't wink
> You can't drink
> You even have to watch what you think.
> You can't have your way
> You can't have much to say
> All you can do is hope and pray.
> There's lots of rules you can plainly see,
> Whitehaven is a _____ of a place to be.
> —Anonymous

Of course, Mr. Eliot wanted to know who Leaping Lena was and also what went in the blank.

Jim and I worked on Thursday nights and Saturdays at Lowenstein's Department Store in downtown Memphis. We would ride the school bus to the city bus stop and ride the city bus to Lowenstein's. Lowenstein's stayed open only on Thursday nights until nine o'clock. One Thursday night after work, Jim and I met to ride the bus, but neither of us had the seven cents for the bus ride. I was depending on him, and he was depending on me. Jim gave me his money and said that he would hitch a ride home. Isn't it wonderful how safe things were in the forties? Neither of us worried about getting home.

I worked in the "Mixing Bowl" department, which was ladies sportswear. I kept something on layaway constantly. After paying about seventy-five cents for lunch on Saturday and keeping something on layaway, I didn't have much money left. I nearly ran my mother crazy every Sunday afternoon, taking my money out of my piggy bank, counting it, and putting it back in the bank. But I am a money-saver. I always would save a portion of what I earned, regardless of how small the amount.

Boys in our graduating class were enlisting in branches of the armed forces just before their eighteenth birthdays so that they could get their choice of the branch of service. We graduated on May 22, 1945, the same year that World War II ended. Jim had joined the navy, and he didn't get to attend our graduation ceremony. All eighteen-year-olds had to register for the service. Just before Roy's eighteenth birthday, he volunteered for the navy. He was assigned to the USS *Uhlman*. His ship was bombed and damaged heavily, and there were some casualties, but they were able to make it to shore. After they docked and were leaving the ship, a young fellow came running to them, asking for his brother. He had not gotten the message that his brother had been killed in the attack. This was only one of the sad occasions that the war brought.

Jim volunteered just before his eighteenth birthday, when he still was a senior in high school, but because his birthday was in March, he didn't miss much of his senior year. He was assigned to the USS *Teaberry*. Since the war was over in August 1945, he didn't have to spend much time in the service.

Roy Jr. and Jim

Everyone probably remembers where they were when they heard the news about the beginning of World War II. Our family had driven to Red Banks, Mississippi, where Daddy had some cattle. Daddy was going to let us children hunt rabbits. Mama stayed by the car because my Uncle Ray and Aunt Tennie were coming to meet us there. When we got back to the car, Aunt Tennie said that while they were riding down, they heard on the radio that the United States had declared war. That was on Sunday, December 7, 1941.

During the next few years, everyone had to make a lot of sacrifices. Food was rationed; shoes were rationed; Roy and Jim joined the navy; and we were stuck with an old car.

One thing we learned was how to budget. I remember that sugar and meat were rationed and probably other food that I have forgotten. Companies quit manufacturing cars. Finally, our car was looking so bad that Jim and Roy decided to give it a good coat of paint with a brush. They chose a putrid green. Our family drove that awful-looking car until companies started manufacturing cars again. That took a lot of courage.

My boyfriend, Thurman, and I had a date at the Peabody Skyway on the night the war was over. When we got to the Skyway, the room was empty. We had not heard that the war was over. Tommy Dorsey's orchestra members and all of the guests had left. Everybody was celebrating in the streets downtown, and we joined them. It was a wonderful feeling.

The following October 5, 1945, Thurman Dewitt Coulter Jr. and I got married. We had a home wedding with about fifty people in attendance. Our only attendants were Buck and Nell Coulter and my little cousin Patsy Nelms as flower girl. A little boy from our church was ring bearer. My aunt May (Patsy's mother) played the wedding march. Brother Flatt, our minister, performed the ceremony.

We spent the first night at the Peabody Hotel, and the next morning we caught the train to Lookout Mountain in Chattanooga, Tennessee. Our transportation? The Frisco Railroad train. Mama and Mrs. Coulter met us at Buntyn Station in Memphis when we returned from our honeymoon.

We lived at my parents' house for quite some time after we were married. Jimmy was born on January 11, 1947—a very beautiful baby boy—while we were still living with my parents. When he was about eighteen months old, we got our first apartment. It was two rooms in a private home with a shared bath. During the war, people made small apartments in their homes to accommodate the many soldiers in our area, and this was one of those apartments. One of the first things I did was to bake a chocolate pie for lunch. Even though I could cook a meal, I had never undertaken a chore like baking a pie. It took me all morning and a messy kitchen to get that pie in the oven—but it was worth it. I never tried to bake again as long as we lived in that tiny apartment because of the small kitchen.

After a few short months, Thurman found us a three-room duplex, which was much better. We later graduated from the duplex to a four-room house next door to Thurman's parents and across and up the street from my parents on Lamar—not the best location, but we got along fairly well.

While we were living on Lamar, I got pregnant with Wayne. Before Wayne was born, Thurman had an accident at work and lost part of his hand. After some time off from work, he went back as superintendent. Wayne was born on October 1, 1950, another very beautiful baby boy. The next year we had our first girl, born on November 25, 1951. She was a very beautiful baby. This was the year that we started looking for a house to buy.

My mother called me one day and asked if I would hold an office in the Missionary Society. The lady who had planned to fill the position was pregnant and didn't feel that she could handle the job. Oh, how I hated to give her my answer because the family didn't know, but there was nothing else I could do. I was pregnant again. Obviously I couldn't handle the job either. We bought a house at 2727 Jeffrey and moved in just before David was born on March 12, 1953, another very beautiful baby boy. At this time we had completed our family—no more surprises.

Since very few families had air conditioners, most of our neighbors spent a lot of time outside. Thurman built a barbeque pit in our backyard, and we spent almost every Saturday night with our neighbors, eating potluck and barbecued chicken. We had such a good time and became a close-knit group.

Eventually, Thurman began to seek female friends outside of our marriage. He also became irritable with me and the children. I will not go into details, but this led to very touchy and physical situations. I came from a loving home, where parents did not mistreat their children or spouses, and I could not and would not get used to this behavior, nor would I subject my children to it.

In January 1958, I was divorced from an abusive

marriage. This was not a quick decision. I had pondered and prayed over this for months and got counseling from my minister, trying to decide if it was better to raise my four children—then ages five, six, seven, and ten—in an abusive situation with two parents or to divorce and raise them with one parent in a safe and secure situation. I chose the latter.

After going to a lawyer and getting the legal aspects worked out, I thought I had better tell Thurman before he got the papers at work. I took the children to my mother's house to spend the night. Then I cooked Thurman's favorite meal, trying to soften the blow in telling him.

After telling Thurman about the divorce, I listened to his excuses, alibis, and promises, all of which I had heard before. His promises lasted about two weeks. The next thing was to tell the children. When they came home, I told them that their dad was going to live with their grandmother and granddaddy. I said that this was a family matter and that they shouldn't tell anyone, but if anyone asked, they should tell them the truth. This all happened on a weekend.

When my daughter, Carolyn, came home from school the next Monday, I noticed that something was bothering her. When I asked her what was wrong, she said, "I know that you told us not to tell about Daddy going to live at Grandmother's house, but I was so excited that I told my teacher."

"What did your teacher say?" I asked. I thought that she gave a good answer. Her teacher had said, "Now you will have two homes."

We lived on child support, which meant scrimping and budgeting. I sewed and made all of Carolyn's and my clothes. I made the boys short-sleeved shirts. I also made costumes for a four-year-old group of children for a dancing studio. I put an ad in the paper and sewed for the public, and I altered pants for a men's store. I would do this to bring in a little extra income. I decided that as the children got older, finances would be even tighter because the children would require more. I needed to make some important decisions about our future.

I started at Memphis State College when I was thirty years old. I would go either on Tuesday and Thursday or on Monday, Wednesday, and Friday. My youngest child, David, was not in school, so I would drop him off at my mother's house on the way to school and pick him up after school, getting there just in time to get him and pick up my other children at Bethel Grove Elementary School.

I would take nine credit hours a semester. I attempted fifteen hours one semester and found that was too much for me to handle. I then dropped back to taking the original nine hours a semester.

One afternoon Thurman called and said, "Do you want to go to Starksville?"

"I can't," I said. "Carolyn is home with the mumps."

He said, "Well, I'm going. Jimmy has gotten hurt." Jimmy was spending two weeks with his aunt Nell and uncle Vernon in Starksville, Mississippi. I called Jim and Grace to see if they could keep Carolyn. Mama and Daddy had taken the boys to see a friend in the country. Before we could start to Starksville, Thurman got a call saying that Nell and Vernon were flying to Memphis, and we were to meet them at the airport. They were sending Jimmy in an ambulance to Campbell's Clinic.

This particular afternoon, Vernon was putting the tractor in the shed, and Jimmy and a neighbor boy were standing on the back of a piece of equipment attached to the tractor. The tractor jerked, and Jimmy fell off. The tire stopped within an inch of Jimmy's head. He was badly hurt. Realizing the seriousness of the accident, Vernon sent the young boy to the house to get a sheet, which he then used to support Jimmy's leg. Jimmy said, "I'm going to lose my leg aren't I, Uncle Vernon?" He too realized how serious the situation was.

Jimmy was rushed to the hospital in Starksville, where they stabilized him, put a splint on his leg, and bandaged two other places that had been cut. Then he was sent in an ambulance with a nurse to Campbell's Clinic in Memphis. We picked up Nell and Vernon at the airport. When we got to the hospital and saw the doctor, he said that he would do everything he could to save the leg but was not making any promises It was about three days before the doctor said that he thought Jimmy was going to be fine. This was in June, and Jimmy stayed in Campbell's Clinic until the last of August, just before school started. He went from crutches to a brace; it was about a year before he was completely well.

The doctor said that when Jimmy was sixteen, he should come back and have some skin grafted over the place where there was no muscle covering the bone, and he was to wear a shield until the skin graft. At the time when he was sixteen, Jimmy was living with his father. I called to remind Thurman what the doctor had recommended, but he chose not to allow Jimmy to have the procedure.

Incidentally, my brother Jim caught the mumps from Carolyn and became desperately ill. He lost three weeks from work.

After a few years of schooling, I really needed a job. I found out that Arkansas school districts were hiring nondegreed teachers with two years of college. My next-door neighbor, Billy Ray, had an aunt who lived in Marked Tree, Arkansas. Billy knew that I had talked about getting a teaching position and, in talking to her niece, learned that there was an opening in Marked Tree. She thought that they were hiring nondegreed teachers. I made an appointment with the superintendent.

The day of my appointment Billy, my friend Millie, and I went to Ruth's house for lunch, and afterward I met with the superintendent. However, he already had hired all of the nondegreed teachers that the law allowed. He called a neighboring town, Lepanto, and the superintendent said that he did have some openings.

I had never heard of Lepanto, but Ruth gave me instructions on how to get there. As I was going in the school, a man was coming out and said that the superintendent was not there. I told him that I was looking for an elementary teaching position and was in a predicament: I couldn't get a job without a degree, and I couldn't get a degree without a job. This man turned out to be Mr. May, the high school counselor. We talked for about thirty minutes.

I couldn't stay until the superintendent returned because I had to get back to Memphis to get my children from school, so I made an agreement with Mr. May—he would tell the superintendent about me, and if he was interested, he would call me that day. If I didn't hear from the superintendant, that would mean he had no openings or just was not interested.

The superintendent called me at four o'clock and said he had three openings—second, third, and fourth grades. I took the middle of the road and was hired over the phone for the third-grade position.

Small towns were something at that time. The superintendent, Mr. McGehee, found me a house to live in and said that I did not need to sign a contract until I started to work; if his word was not any good, a contract would not be either. I was hired for twenty-four hundred dollars a year, with a stipulation that I get twelve college hours each year until I had earned my bachelor's degree. When school started, I got a three hundred dollar raise.

This was one of the best decisions I ever made.

We moved to Lepanto on August 1, 1962. It seemed like we were going back in time. Telephones still had operators that talked to you. No one gave directions by using house numbers. When anyone asked where we lived, we learned to say, "Where the Coopers used to live;" and everyone knew where that was. It was an entirely different atmosphere than living in Memphis. I just loved it.

After we had been in Lepanto about a week, we invited two of the children's friends from Memphis, Chuck and Tommy Epperson, to spend a few days with us. The children were playing outside when Tommy tried to jump across a small ditch and fell on a stone that was lining a driveway. He had a pretty big gash on his leg. I knew that he'd have to have stitches. I picked up the phone and told the operator that I was new in town and needed a doctor and told her why.

"I'll call you back," she said. When she did, she said, "I couldn't reach Dr. Oates, but I'll see if I can get Dr. Jones—if he's not drunk."

I talked to Tommy's mother, and she decided that he could finish his visit with us. When he returned to Memphis, he saw their family doctor, who said that Dr. Jones had done a fine job.

The children had been a little reluctant about leaving Memphis and their friends, so we made a trip to Memphis at least once a week. That lasted until school started, and they made friends at school and got involved in school activities. The Memphis trips became farther and farther apart.

Our first year in Lepanto went well. Wayne, Carolyn, and David made new friends and adjusted well to their new life. My first year was rather strenuous, with a very negative principal. School was out in May, and I had to make arrangements to take my twelve college hours in order for my contract to be renewed. I enrolled in Memphis State. I would leave Lepanto on Sunday nights and take the children to my parents' house. My father would follow me to my dorm. I got out of school early on Friday, so I would get the children and be on my way to Lepanto.

I would do the laundry and get us ready for the next week, and the routine would start all over again. Each summer semester would last five weeks, so that didn't leave much vacation time. After two years of the routine, I transferred to Arkansas State College. I could stay at home and drive back and forth to Jonesboro.

There was a car pool going to Jonesboro during the summer, six of us in one car. It put me in the front middle seat, sitting on the bump. We would leave about six in the morning and get home around noon. The children were at the age of sleeping until noon. Wayne was fifteen, Carolyn was fourteen, and David was thirteen years old. They had graduated from having babysitters and were typical teenagers. Jimmy was still living in Memphis with his dad.

Twelve hours a year was really, really a slow process. I decided to ask my superintendent for a year's leave of absence. I would graduate in that length of time if I went full time. My superintendent, Mr. Langrell, granted me permission. Another teacher and I took a year off and got our degrees. In order for me to take a year's leave, we moved into government housing. We had a nice three-bedroom duplex with living room, dining area, kitchen, laundry area, and one bathroom—very adequate for my family. We were back living on child support, and I was going to school on a government loan.

I got a loan that would pay my annual payments if I taught in a poverty school. Lepanto was considered a poverty school. At the end of every year, I would receive an application to fill out, which needed Mr. Langrell's signature. Then I'd return it to the college, and that would be my annual payment. My entire loan was paid by teaching in a poverty school.

In August 1966, I received my bachelor of science in education from Arkansas State College. My salary was $4,400 annually, which made all of the hard work well worth it. We thought we were rich.

In the summer of 1964, Carolyn and I were coming from Memphis when she saw Bill Hudgens on the opposite side of the interstate, having car trouble. We turned around, but by the time we reached his car, Bill was not there. We later learned that someone had taken him to West Memphis to get help. That night, Bill called because he thought that we might have come back to help. While we were talking, Bill said, "Let's go get a cup of coffee." From that time on, we probably drank more coffee than anyone in town, but it was the beginning of a long and beautiful friendship.

Bill was the high school science teacher and federal coordinator. He was the organist and choir director at the Methodist church. Since we both taught school, we attended most school functions together. In fact, our first date was to an out-of-town football game in Gosnell, Arkansas

On March 4, 1967, I became a proud grandmother. James Troy Coulter was born to Jimmy and Betty Coulter. Jimmy, my oldest son, had spent his teenage years living with his dad and stepmother in Memphis, and he married Betty Isbell right out of high school. Bill and I went to Memphis to get a glimpse of the baby through the glass window of the hospital nursery. This was the beginning of a long line of grandchildren, great-grandchildren, and great-great-grandchildren.

Now that I was working, I had to move from the government housing. It was very difficult to find a rental house in a small town, but I finally found a nice-looking sizable house—but looks can be deceiving. The owner had added a den to the kitchen. It sloped to the back, and if you dropped a ball or even a potato, it would roll down the floor to the end wall. When it rained, we had to put containers to catch the rain and then empty them every so often. The owner attempted to fix the problem once but failed. Obviously, we never got to use the den. This was house number three.

Another rental house became available across from the high school, and we took it. This was our fourth Lepanto house, and we hoped that we could stay there. We liked the house and the location. During this segment of my life, Wayne graduated from high school and started to college. Wayne had always been the shortest one in his class, including the girls. He was going to school in Senatobia, Mississippi. Bill would go get him almost every weekend, bring him home, and then take him back. Every weekend I would spend my time letting the hem out of his pants. He was finally growing. Carolyn was a busy senior, and David was a tenth-grader.

We only had one car, and it stayed very, very busy. It was really good because the children did the grocery shopping, delivered my monthly payments, and ran errands. One afternoon I had some of the teachers over for coffee. While we were drinking coffee at the kitchen table, the gas man arrived.

"I'm here to light your pilots," he said.

"Come in," I said. "Why do you have to light my pilots?"

"The gas was turned off."

"Why was the gas turned off?" I asked.

"You are Gertrude Coulter, aren't you?" the gas man said.

"Yes."

The gas man hesitated a moment and then said, "Uh, your gas bill wasn't paid."

This young man was trying so hard not to tell the whole story in front of my guests, but I was persistent. This is what happened: whoever was supposed to pay the gas bill when it was due failed to do so, and the gas was cut off. David was driving around town after school, saw the bill on the front seat, and stopped by City Hall to pay it—and the gas was turned on. This went on while I was drinking coffee with my colleagues.

There had been rumors going around town that my landlord was moving back to Lepanto. I hoped that was untrue—it would mean she'd want the house. I had heard nothing—but then my landlord called and said that she was moving back and wanted her house by the first of the month. When the first of the month came, no rental house was available. I stored my furniture, and each one of us stayed with different friends until a house became available. It was a four-room, one-bathroom house. We crammed our furniture in and lived there until another more suitable house became available. This was house number five.

It was a very busy year. Wayne and his girlfriend, Sandy, got married; I had two new grandbabies; I attended a three-week workshop; and my father passed away.

I attended an Adult Education Workshop in Morehead, Kentucky, during the summer of 1971, and it inspired me to get my master's degree. I worked on my master's in reading during the summer and took some night courses. My superintendent had suggested that I take my electives in elementary administration, which I did. I received my master's degree in education in August 1974.

After school, I would drive to Memphis to eat with my parents. Mama always cooked me a good meal. When I was leaving after one such visit, Daddy handed me a five-dollar bill; he always thought that he had to give me some money whenever he saw me, and I always accepted it. The next morning, after I had arrived at school, I got a message that my dad had had a heart attack, and I was to go to the Methodist Hospital in Memphis. That five dollars that my dad gave me paid for the gas to get me to Memphis. Ironic, isn't it? When I got to the hospital, I had a message to go to my mother's, which told me that my dad's heart attack was fatal. He was buried on October 21, 1971, at Memorial Park Cemetery in Memphis.

My dad was truly a family man. He was a good husband, father, and grandfather. He and my mother provided my brothers and me with a loving and stable home. My mother relied on her Christian faith and her family to get her through this tragedy.

We all miss him and always will.

Roy Sr. and Gertie Shapard

Over the next year, a lot happened at home. Carolyn got engaged to Larry Ashley, and we planned their wedding. I made the bridesmaids' dresses—a very time-consuming project. A week before the wedding, a rental house became available. As much as we needed a larger house, the timing was off, but we rented the house. In one week's time, we moved and got the house presentable for out-of-town guests who were coming to the house after the wedding. You can get a lot done under pressure when you are young and have some good friends. This was house number six.

I taught remedial reading and helped classroom teachers with their slow readers. Chapter 1 equipped the reading lab with excellent materials and equipment. I also started a basic education night class for adults. I could use my reading lab materials for the class. It was amazing how many people attended. It was also rewarding. A student about my age came in one night, so excited. He said, "I wrote my first check today."

In the spring of 1976, the school board hired me as elementary principal for the 1976–77 school year, with the stipulation that I get my administration certification. Back to school again. My first year as principal went well, mainly because I had the backing of my most efficient faculty. Together, we had a very good year. I got my certification before the next school year began. Hopefully, there would be no more school for me.

Wayne and Sandy had been living on campus at Arkansas State University and had just bought a new trailer. They were home in Lepanto one weekend when they got the news that a tornado had struck Jonesboro. They returned to find their home in shambles; it was twisted in the middle. The end that was upside down was Tanya's bedroom and the bathroom. Have you ever been hit on the head with a toilet seat? The bathroom facilities were literally hanging upside down. The other half of the trailer was perfectly intact. Pictures were still on the wall in the living room. They had been hung with scotch tape because Sandy didn't want to have any nail holes in the wall. Wayne's wedding ring was found in the field next to their trailer, still in the soap dish where he had put it. Every piece of wearing apparel had to be washed or cleaned. They piled all of the clothes in my carport; and Janie and I washed and cleaned them while the kids cleaned out their trailer. There is always something to be thankful for. I am so thankful that the kids were in Lepanto when the tornado hit and not in Jonesboro.

Wayne graduated from Arkansas State University, and he, Sandy, and Tanya moved back to Lepanto. They found a house for rent, but the owner did not want to accept children. I agreed to move into that house (number seven) and let them have house number six. Number seven was an older house with a glassed front porch and large rooms and was partly furnished. This arrangement worked out fine for all of us.

School was closed on January 3, 1977, because of snow. Just as Bill and I finished supper, Wayne came in to tell us that Jim had had a heart attack. We immediately went to my mother's in Memphis. Jim had been jogging and had come in to talk on the phone. He then went to the carport to cool down. When someone went to call him to supper, they found him passed out. He was rushed to the hospital, but it was too late. I lost my best friend. We had grown up together, rather close for a sister and brother but twins are like that. This was a great loss to the entire family, especially his immediate family. Danny had just had a new baby son, and Karen was only sixteen years old, which is a crucial age to lose a parent.

David was working in Helena, Arkansas, and Carolyn and Larry were living in West Memphis and expecting their first child. Jimmy and Betty were in Memphis and had three children. Time was really flying.

I was sitting in my office one Friday afternoon when the phone rang. It was Shirley, Roy's wife. She said, "Sister, can you take Pam?" Pam, my niece, had been staying in Texas with Shirley's brother, but he was unable to keep her any longer. Roy was a captain for American Airlines and was out of town. Shirley wanted to get Pam situated before he returned home. My next question was when. I picked up Pam at the airport the next morning, and that weekend we got her ready to start school on Monday morning.

Friends can be so influential on teenagers, and Pam had some friends in Connecticut that had a negative influence on her. She was now in Lepanto and was making new friends. She graduated from Lepanto High School. Pam is so smart and made a positive change in her life. She went to college and now has a fabulous job working overseas for a US company.

One afternoon I was having my after-school cup of coffee at my kitchen table, and I thought, *I wonder how much principals in West Memphis make.* I got up and called the superintendent's office and made an appointment. I had no intention of moving; I just wanted to know how my salary compared to those in West Memphis. After talking to the superintendent, I learned that elementary principals made four thousand dollars more than I did. That sounded like a fortune, even though it was only sixteen thousand dollars—salaries were very low in 1979 compared to salaries of today.

The very next week Carolyn called and said that the principal at Bragg Elementary School in West Memphis was retiring. My superintendent had just passed out intent papers for the following year. They were due in his office the following Monday. On Friday, I called Mr. Kessinger, West Memphis superintendent, and asked if I was in the running for the principal's job. He said that I was and asked if he could call my superintendent. I told him to wait until Monday; I had to get there first.

In six weeks, I had closed out the school in Lepanto, had a new job in West Memphis, and moved into an apartment in West Memphis. This was the first time that I had lived in an apartment, and I thoroughly enjoyed it. I thought that I would never want to live in a house again. Life was moving fast.

It was really sad, leaving Lepanto. I had started my career, made many friends, and raised my children there. A small town is the best place to raise children. If I needed to find one of my children, I would call the Dairy Freeze. The owners had put a phone on the outside, and the children answered it. One night Wayne was late coming home, so I called the Dairy Freeze. Butch Donham answered the phone. I asked if Wayne was there. Butch said, "No, ma'am, he rode out the highway with a friend, but your car is here. Do you need it?" That was so characteristic of Lepanto.

I started to work in West Memphis on August 1, 1979. There was really a lot for me to learn about the new school. I didn't know the teachers or students. I met one of the teachers who lived in the apartment complex where I lived. A few of the teachers stopped by the school to meet me before school started, and I was thankful for that.

I had a very efficient and knowledgeable faculty. I had a secretary who helped me, and I could not have gotten through the first year without her. When I was placing children in their classrooms, Von tactfully told me that I had mixed my fifth- and sixth-graders. Some of the children might have appreciated my promoting them to the sixth grade, but the ones that I was demoting would not. Von straightened me out on that issue.

On the home front, Carolyn had our family Thanksgiving dinner at her house. My nephew Paul Shapard, his wife, and their three boys had just moved to Southaven, Mississippi, and had Thanksgiving with our family. Kindergarten in Southaven was not mandatory at that time, and Billy was kindergarten age. I offered to keep Billy during the week so that he could go to kindergarten at Bragg Elementary, where I was principal. I would get him on Sunday, and his daddy would pick him up on Friday. That worked well for us all.

My first year at Bragg went rather smoothly. I missed the faculty at Lepanto, but the Lepanto secretary kept in touch. Von kept me informed about Bragg. I had a congenial and efficient faculty, which is the bright spot in any job. I knew that I had made the right move. I was at Bragg seven years before I was promoted to elementary supervisor. I moved from Bragg to the central office. While in the central office, I accomplished some really important issues. I was instrumental in getting the elementary schools through North Central and also in starting the HIPPY program (Home Improvement Program for Preschool Youngsters).

I was sent to Israel to the Hebrew University to learn all of the aspects of the program. When I came home,

I started it at Jackson Elementary School. Parents were taught how to teach their preschool children so that when they started school, they would be more ready to learn.

The first group of children who went through the program was put in the same first grade class when they started school, and they stayed together for two years. By the time the class reached second grade, only about a third of the HIPPY class still attended school at Jackson. This process proved that parental help and attention at home is essential to a child's progress in school.

Family update: Wayne, Sandy, and Tanya moved to West Memphis. Carolyn and Larry had one daughter. David moved to Texas. Jimmy and Betty now had four children—two boys and two girls.

The year 1984 was a bad one for my mother. She broke her hip, had a ruptured appendix, and broke her arm. After getting out of the hospital with her broken hip, she came to my house in West Memphis. Even though I loved my apartment living, I had bought a small house in West Memphis with a pool. Regrets! Regrets! Regrets! It was difficult caring for my mother and working and caring for a house with a pool. The pool was the one that was neglected.

In the summer of the same year, Mama had a ruptured appendix. She was so sick that I thought that she was not going to pull through. I had the month of July off, so I stayed with her when she was released from the hospital. Every day her open wound had to be irrigated and dressed. I learned some nursing skills, and Grace came over often to help out. By the time I had to return to work, Mama was able to stay by herself. She was not able to cook, so I fixed enough TV dinners to last her through the week. This worked out fairly well.

In December, Betty took her to the doctor, and Mama fell at the curb and broke her arm. She was in the hospital and therapy through Christmas and her birthday in January. By now she was not able to stay by herself. I got a lady from West Memphis to stay with her during the week, and I stayed on weekends. Doll would call me on Friday with the grocery list, and I would take their groceries and bring Doll back to West Memphis. Doll stayed with Mama for about two years.

We got another lady through the Salvation Army. Betty Jean was glad to have a place to stay because she had just been put out of her son's house. We had the same routine—I still stayed on weekends. On Sunday, January 24, we celebrated Mama's eighty-eighth birthday. Most family members were there, and she seemed to be feeling good—as good as an eighty-eight-year-old can. On Wednesday, she passed away.

Mama had a good life. She was a devout Christian and attended church services and circle meetings as long as she could drive. I miss her, and I guess I always will. Now, only Roy and I were left in the immediate family, and he lived in Connecticut.

While I was staying in Memphis, taking care of business, I decided that if the school board would okay my living in Memphis, I would move into Mama's house and sell mine in West Memphis. I would have no monthly house payments, and it was a larger and much nicer house than mine in West Memphis. Mr. Kessinger gave me the okay for living out of town. I drove back and forth from Memphis to West Memphis until I retired in 1992.

Another tragedy struck our family on November 21, 1991. Roy was shot and killed as he was returning home. He was left in his yard to die. This incident created a tremendous amount of publicity during the capture and trial of the perpetrator. All of the news that this created would have embarrassed Roy because he was a very private person. He was a quiet, sophisticated person. Now, I was the only one left in my immediate family. I will always miss my family.

I retired from West Memphis School District on June 30, 1992. This was a sweet and sour occasion. I was happy to be retiring, but I would miss all of my friends that I had been working with the last few years. The elementary schools gave me a great send-off. I had four send-off parties and was given a complete set of luggage. The office force had a luncheon for me and another retiree, and we were given an envelope of money. All in all, I had a great and sad send-off.

To wean me from my school mentality, I volunteered in the Memphis city schools one morning a week, helping students who were behind in their schoolwork. One first grader that I worked with could not remember what she had worked on the week before, yet she could not be tested for special education or be retained because of district rules. I often wonder what happened to her.

The second year I worked at Magnolia Elementary School. When I arrived the first day, I was sent to the teacher workroom for a gathering of the tutors. Several of us who were tutoring that day met and introduced ourselves. After I introduced myself, one of the teachers came over to me and asked if I was David and Carolyn's mother. It was Imogene Moore. Imogene had babysat for me when my children were just babies. I had Imogene over for lunch and invited Carolyn and Wayne; David was in St. Thomas. We had a glorious reunion. I am sure Imogene is just as good a teacher as she was a babysitter.

One of the things that I had always wanted to do was go camping, but it seemed that I could never afford it or never had the time. I started looking for campers. I found one that I thought was a good beginner camper. Wayne, Tanya, and I went to look at it, and it got a pass from all of us. Wayne and I agreed to swap vehicles when I went camping because he had a truck. The camper was a Hi-Lo—easy to pull and easy to handle. It raised and lowered at the push of a button. What could be better than that? Well, driving and parking were two different things. Jimmy took me to a church parking lot and tried to teach me how to back up. I learned at the moment, but it kind of faded when I tried to back into my driveway—it took a long, long time.

Grace, Helen, and I went on our maiden voyage, as we called it, to Arkabutla, Mississippi. That was a hilarious trip. I learned from that trip to get a pull-through so that I wouldn't have to back up. We did get set up and really enjoyed our weekend camping trip. Here are some of the things that happened: we couldn't get started when we began to leave because we hadn't removed the stabilizers. The camp ranger had to tell us what was wrong. As we started out, we took the wrong turn and had to turn around to get back on track. Yes, I said turn around. It took us forever to get turned around, but one thing we had was patience and humor. We finally got turned around and were on our way home. When we got home, and I was trying to back into the driveway, a good Samarian came along and backed the camper in for me. One thing about little old ladies and camping: they nearly always get help. I guess people thought we look like we needed it, and we did. But we have perseverance and patience, and it takes a whole of both.

While I still had the Hi-Lo, Grace and I decided to go to Orlando for a winter vacation. We made reservations at a campground, and after a two-day trip, we arrived at our campground. We pushed the button to raise the top of the camper—and nothing happened. All of our things were in the camper, and we couldn't get in. Since it was so late, we decided to stay at a motel for the night and deal with the camper the next morning. It took all the next day to get the camper fixed and get back in our camping spot. After we had been there about a week, we returned to our camper after our daily excursion and found that the refrigerator had stopped working. We decided that instead of buying a portable refrigerator we would just buy ice each day, and that worked for us.

We took several side trips, went to Disney World, and all in all had a wonderful time. When it was time to go back to Tennessee, we checked with the state police to see about the roads from Orlando to Memphis. We had heard that there had been some ice and snow in Memphis. The state police said that the roads were clear, so we started on our journey home. The roads, however, were not clear. We ran into frozen snow and one-lane traffic. We were driving in ruts and going the speed of the car in front of us. We couldn't get off the highway because we didn't know the condition of the roads or the ramps. When we got to Oxford, we saw a motel, and we stopped. We got the last available room. The place was full because the Mississippi State Police had told most of the people the same thing they told us. The next morning the roads to Memphis had cleared, and we made our way home safely. We were glad to be home.

Since we had so much trouble with my Hi-Lo camper, I decided to shop for another camper. I purchased a twenty-seven-foot Dutchman travel trailer, quite a step up from the Hi-Lo. I didn't take any long trips in this camper but did take quite a few short trips. We spent a lot of time in Mountain View, Arkansas, and Mississippi and Tennessee state parks.

My Dutchman camper

One of the most hurtful things for a mother is to lose a child, and this has been the hardest thing that I have written. On September 8, 1998, Wayne had one kidney removed because of cancer. He came through with flying colors. He came home from the hospital on September 10, and in a week, he was back to work. On one of our lunch visits, he told me that when he first knew that he had cancer, he took a gun that Tanya's grandfather had given him and gave it to Seth. He wanted it to stay in the family. He laughed and said, "Now that I am going to be all right, I wish that I hadn't given it away."

In November 2000, Grace and I were visiting David in St. Thomas. As we were drinking our morning coffee, David showed us an e-mail from Wayne. His cancer had returned, this time in his lungs. He said the tumor was about the size of a grapefruit. His surgery was scheduled for December 4. We were scheduled to leave for home in two days and so would be home for his surgery. Our vacation mood quickly left us, and we were anxious to catch our plane.

Wayne was in the hospital for four days after his surgery. The doctor said that the surgery went well. The next October, he was scheduled for a CAT scan, and it looked like he needed another lung surgery. He was under the care of Dr. Weeks with the Family Cancer Center. Wayne had his second lung surgery on October 30, 2001. He came home from the hospital on November 6.

Wayne decided to go to West Clinic. His doctor was Dr. Tauer. Dr. Tauer did everything he could for Wayne, and Wayne was a fighter. He was in and out of the hospital until May. Then, I took him to Baptist East for blood about twice a week and to West Clinic twice a week for chemo.

On May 27, Wayne went to Tanya's for a week. They fixed the back of Tanya's SUV so that he could lie down, and he was on his way. Even though he was very sick, he enjoyed every minute, and I was so glad that he got to spend that week with Tanya and her family. Tanya had been coming every weekend for months. Ann, Wayne's friend, brought him home from Tanya's.

The day after he returned from Tanya's, Bill and I took him to Baptist East for blood, but instead, he was admitted to the hospital. As Bill and I drove home from the hospital, I told him, "I know we won't bring him home."

On Friday, June 7, I spent the day at the hospital. I talked to Wayne and told him that Tanya would be there soon. He said, "Is it urgent?"

"It's Friday," I told him. "Tanya comes every Friday."

When Tanya and Ann got to the hospital, Ann brought me home.

I had just gotten in bed when Carolyn called and said that Tanya had called for us to go back to the hospital. We were at the hospital all night. On Saturday morning, family was in and out. Wayne passed away around noon on Saturday, with Tanya, Ann, Carolyn, and me at his bedside.

My third camper was the same size as the Dutchman, except that my new one was a fifth-wheel and had a slide-out. This was my favorite camper because it was so much easier to pull, and the slide-out made more room inside. By now, I was spending my camping time in Mountain View. It was about a three-hour drive from Memphis, and there was a lot of activity there. We liked to go to town and listen to different groups play and sing bluegrass music. It was like going back in time. The last two years that I had my camper, I left it in Mountain View for the summer and camped a few days at a time. When I had my eightleth birthday, I decided to give it up. I didn't want the responsibility of keeping it. Also, I didn't think that an eighty-year-old female needed to be driving a camper. However, I have missed my camper very much and think maybe I was a little premature in my decision.

When I still had the camper, Ann and I decided on the spur of the moment that we would go camping. It was Friday, and she was off for the weekend. I had my paper delivery stopped for Friday and Saturday. We left Friday afternoon and went to Mountain View, Arkansas. We had a nice weekend and returned home on Sunday afternoon. When I started to unlock the back door, it was already unlocked. I wondered if some of the family had been there, but as we entered the house, we immediately knew that it was not family. Wayne had told me that I needed to get an alarm system, but the police said at a Neighborhood Watch meeting that window guards were sufficient. I guess Wayne knew more that the police.

The intruders had pried the window guard off my back bedroom window, broken a window pane, reached in, and unlocked the window. They had a ball in my bedroom. They took money and rings from my chest of drawers and costume jewelry from my vanity. I kept a smiley-face cookie jar on top of my chest of drawers and kept all of my change in it. At Christmas, all of the grandchildren and some of the grown children drew from the cookie jar. They would count their money, and the one with the most money would get to draw again. The robbers were very neat. They took a pillowcase off my bed, emptied the money from old smiley-face in the pillowcase, and left the cookie jar. I was so glad for their thoughtfulness. In my computer room, I had left a watch on my desk that my mother had gotten for her sixteenth birthday, and they took that. I had taken it out to get it fixed for Carolyn's Christmas. They had also taken a ring that belonged to my grandfather's sister. These two heirlooms were irreplaceable.

From that time on, I never had my paper delivery stopped. The paper man knew that I was going to be gone Friday and Saturday nights. The house was broken into on Friday night. I searched all of the pawn shops in the neighborhood but found none of my belongings. On Monday morning, I called ADT, the home security company, and they came the next day and installed an alarm system.

Wayne's house had been vacant for two years, and Carolyn and Tanya had been trying to convince me that I needed to move to West Memphis. I hesitated because I was living in the house that my mother and father had built, and it was practically maintenance-free. I loved the house. I knew that I probably needed to be in West Memphis, so I finally gave in, sold my house in Memphis, and moved into Wayne's house in West Memphis. Even though I had worked and lived in West Memphis before, I knew only people who were connected to the school system, and I had been retired for twelve years. So I told Carolyn and Jimmy that I would make the move, but they would have to move me.

So here I am in West Memphis. The furniture in my house is just where they placed it when they moved it, and it will probably stay there as long as I live here—another move, another house.

However, I am content in West Memphis. Every Thursday I have lunch and play Rummikues with friends. I go to Silver Sneakers exercise class once a week. I attend our class luncheon every fourth Monday. In between, I slip off to the casino and have lunch. I stay pretty busy, keeping up with my health and beauty appointments. All in all, I am right where I want and need to be.

Bill and I had been friends with a particular couple for years. Al and Trish lived in Conway, Arkansas, and every few months we would meet somewhere between Conway and West Memphis for lunch. On the night of August 23, 2012, Bill and I were trying to set a date to meet Al and Trish. The next day I had a doctor's appointment in Memphis. As I was attempting to park the car for my appointment, Melinda Hannah called to tell me that Bill had had a fatal heart attack. It probably had happened the night before, but he was found that morning. This was such a shock because I had just talked to him the night before, and he seemed fine. This was also a shock to the town of Lepanto because he was such a prominent member of the community. I lost my best friend, but I know that Wayne and Bill are rejoicing together in heaven. I can just hear Wayne saying, "Bill, what are you doing here?" And Bill answering, "Just checking on you."

On Friday, May 15, 2015, the Whitehaven class of '45 gathered to celebrate the seventieth anniversary of their graduation that took place May 22, 1945. On that day, ninety-six students had marched across the stage at Whitehaven High School to receive their hard-earned diplomas, and in 2015, sixteen of those graduates were on hand to celebrate their reunion. Five of them were accompanied by one of their children—these people were nearing ninety years old. Even though some were in wheelchairs or using walkers, all had broad smiles and positive attitudes as they promised to gather again in five years for a seventy-fifth reunion. After our fiftieth reunion, the class started meeting every fourth Monday for lunch. We started with good group attendance, but it has dwindled. Now, it's good if we have five or six in attendance, but we are hanging in there, and some of us have said we would still meet if there were only two of us left. We still have that school spirit.

Things have changed drastically since I was a child. Fear has overtaken contentment; homes are one-parent homes; mothers work outside of the home; children ride busses to school instead of walking. Electronics have taken over, and I have gotten right in the thick of it. I couldn't do without my TV, or my cell phone, or my computer, or my laptop, or my Kindle, or my iPad. I guess you might say that I am hooked. When I was growing up, however,

I didn't need any electronics. We were content with a dial phone and a radio.

I do enjoy relaxing and watching a good TV program. I enjoy being able to see my former students, friends, and family on Facebook. I won't go out of the house without my cell phone because someone just might call me. I like being able to text or e-mail someone. I am enjoying all the changes that society has provided, yet I still think that I grew up in the best of times.

The Coulter Clan—Wayne, Carolyn, David, Jimmy

Made in the USA
Coppell, TX
08 January 2022

71191617R00038